Cavalier and Puritan Fashions

Tom Tierney

Dover Publications, Inc.
Mineola, New York

Introduction

Puritanism emerged during the late sixteenth and seventeenth centuries as a movement to reform or "purify" the perceived corruption and decadence of the Roman Catholic Church in England. By publicly questioning church practices, Martin Luther (1483–1546), a German priest, was instrumental in establishing the Protestant Reformation movement, which spread throughout northern Europe, prompting bitter feuding and persecution between the two religions in countries such as England and France. From this controversy the Puritans emerged, an English sect that promoted the notion of a covenant relationship with God, and maintained an austere lifestyle free of the trappings of the Catholic Church. English Protestants, including the Puritans, struggled for decades to win their right to worship, which was granted and revoked with the whim of each succeeding monarch. In France, the Protestants (known as Huguenots), were similarly repressed by the government, prompting their own civil wars for decades until the Edict of Nantes was adopted, protecting religious worship. However, the revocation of the Edict by Louis XIV in 1685, forced them to flee to tolerant countries like Holland and Switzerland for safety and asylum.

The Puritan movement to the New World began in 1620, when an English "Separatist" faction who wanted to worship outside of the established Anglican Church obtained permission to start a new English settlement across the Atlantic. Because of their long journey, they were also known as "Pilgrims." Those Puritans who sailed to America on the *Mayflower* took with them their austere way of living and dressing, and the harsh conditions of frontier life aided in maintaining that simplicity.

Fashions during this time were greatly influenced by foreign trends and available textiles. The predominantly Protestant Dutch merchant class taste for simpler, less cumbersome, dress styles were a great influence on the Puritans' garb. There were three distinct types of dress worn in Holland: court dress which closely followed the latest French fashions, the "regent" class of wealthy merchants and political leaders who preferred somber black clothes as a mark of their sober pious authority, and finally the common folk, who wore bits and pieces of used clothing previously worn by the upper classes.

Under Louis XIII, France had established itself as the fashion arbiter of the world and it was under his reign (1610–1643) that the "Cavalier" style first came into vogue. Across the channel in England, the padded stiffness of the Elizabethan era was replaced by a more casual, romantic look. The simpler lines of the clothing for both men and women were reflected in plain but rich fabrics. During the Restoration Period in England (1660–1685), people sought to put the severity of Puritan fashions behind as they became more stylishly dressed. Lace and brightly colored ribbons were used in abundance on luxurious fabrics, adorning just about any surface that would hold them. English Restoration fashions and the fashions of the court of Louis XIV were almost interchangeable.

Bibliographical Note

Cavalier and Puritan Fashions is a new work, first published by Dover Publications, Inc., in 2005.

DOVER *Pictorial Archive* SERIES

International Standard Book Number: 0-486-43655-1

Manufactured in the United States of America
Dover Publications, Inc., 31 East 2nd Street, Mineola, N.Y. 11501

English-American Puritans, ca. 1635

Above is a typical representation of the early Puritan settlers who came over on the *Mayflower* in 1620. Puritans of both sexes were known for their somber clothing, as well as the men's distinctive tall black hats. Contrary to modern-day belief, the Puritans wore other dark colors besides black, although the collars and cuffs were always white. Garments during this time were simpler versions of court dress, but strict Puritans avoided court ornamentation such as ribbon or embroidery. On occasion, however, a particularly pious Puritan would wear undergarments that were neatly stitched with Bible verses.

Martin Luther, ca. 1530

This illustration was rendered from a painting of Martin Luther. In 1517, disturbed by the practice of indulgences, which allowed people to offer money as penance for their sins, Luther wrote a series of short opinions to challenge the corruption of the Catholic Church. He supposedly nailed these "Ninety-Five Theses," as they were called, to the door of a church, and they were quickly copied and circulated among the community and later, the continent. He was excommunicated from the Catholic Church by the pope in 1521, and later created an evangelical church calling for reformation of the Christian faith. In images such as these, Luther is generally depicted in dark robes.

English officer and Pilgrim farmers from Jamestown, ca. 1610
Founded on May 14, 1607, Jamestown was the first permanent English settlement established
in North America. Named after King James I, the colony was led by military officers who were
generally noblemen, as depicted by the figure on the right. However, the majority of the
colonists were a lower class of farmers who often had Puritan leanings.

French Huguenot refugees flee to Holland, ca. 1620

The French Huguenots were a prosperous and industrious Protestant group whose persecution began in 1523 with the burning of the martyr Jean Vallière. Though harassed by the French government, especially under Louis XIV, the Protestant movement continued to grow. Many Huguenots fled to other parts of Europe and America for safety and relative freedom. A Huguenot couple is depicted here, during a time of peaceable prosperity. The gentleman wears paned trunk hose over canions with a ribbon garter, with a falling or soft ruff at the neck, and a large brimmed beaver or felt hat. The lady wears a wired cap and collar, with her outer skirt tucked up to reveal her petticoat. Muted colors were common, such as browns, grays, deep greens, and blues, accented with white collars and cuffs.

Dutch aristocrats in court dress, ca. 1620

Through the Twelve Years' Truce of 1609, Holland gained her freedom from Spain, becoming a parliamentary monarchy. At the time, the Dutch aristocracy still looked to France for fashion influences, while the French, in turn, were inspired by the Spanish styles. This couple is dressed in the Spanish mode, which gave prominence to dark, somber colors, accented with white cuffs and collars.

Dutch townspeople, ca. 1620

The Dutch middle class wore simplified versions of aristocratic clothing, without the elaborate ornamentation of court gowns and outfits. Since the practice of making ready-to-wear clothing had not yet begun, all garments were handmade to order. The used-clothing trade was a brisk one for the middle class, while the lower classes made their own clothes from the patterns of those second-generation pieces. This man wears full-cut breeches (often referred to as Dutch slops), an unpadded doublet, and a sleeveless jerkin over his shirt. The woman wears a tightly fitted bodice, a full skirt with a large apron tied under the bodice, and a pleated collar and cuffs. Her cap is wired to fit closely around her face.

Dutch regent and wife, ca. 1620–30

Members of the regent class were responsible for managing the Dutch parliamentary government. As successful merchants, they preferred a less ostentatious look than that of the royals, though they indulged in rich fabrics, generally in dark colors. Being very conservative, they clung to the large ruffs of the previous century, known as "millstone ruffs." The sober fashions of the regents served as a model for the modest Puritan refugees who had fled to Holland.

King Charles I and Queen Henrietta Maria, ca. 1630

The reign of King Charles I (1600–1649) of England and his wife Henrietta Maria (1609–1669), which lasted from 1625–1649, was marked by dissent for his authoritative rule, which he justified by the idea of divine right for the British monarchs. Charles became the enemy of the Protestant Parliament and an eventual victim of the English civil wars. Due in part to the influence of his French wife, who was sister to King Louis XIII, the fashions of Charles's court were based on the French cavalier trend. Typical outfits included pastel tones heavily decorated with gold embroidery, lace, and ribbons.

French cavaliers, ca. 1630

Derived from the Latin word for horseman, the term "cavalier" was applied to the followers of Charles I and his royalist cause. As a fashion trend, it emphasized a dashing, adventurous look and spread all over Europe, including France and Holland. The style featured shorter jackets, rich fabrics and trims in flamboyant colors, broad hats with flowing plumes, and wide-topped boots.

Dutch upper-middle-class lady, ca. 1630

Due to its brisk trade and shipping industries, Holland had become the most prosperous country in the world by the 1630s. The Dutch cavalier look was more restrained than that of other countries, with simpler lines and elegant fabrics. The young lady wears a gown of pale satin and a bodice with elbow-length sleeves. Although the stomacher was out of fashion in the rest of Europe, this gown has a vestigial one outlined by lace trim.

Dutch cavalier, ca. 1630

This young gallant is in the military and wears a steel breastplate over a knitted jerkin and shirt. His Rheingraves, also known as petticoat breeches, are wide-cut culottes, and his accessories include a plumed hat and bucket-topped boots. Fawn, tan, and other warm colors were popular for men at this time.

English upper-middle-class Protestants, ca. 1645

Many English Protestants were sympathetic toward the Puritan and Parliamentarian cause, since they shared similar beliefs. They adopted the basic look of the Puritan costume, but did not follow their rules of strict simplicity and adapted the fashion to suit their preferences. For example, although elements of the Puritan costume can be seen here, the lady's open gown and brightly patterned underskirt would not meet strict Puritanical standards, and the man's ribbons at throat and knee would be considered frivolous.

English merchant-class townsfolk, ca. 1645–50

These Protestant townsfolk are wearing Puritan-inspired fashions to demonstrate their allegiance to the Parliamentary Protestant cause. The lady carries a fur muff, which was popular with both men and women at this time. Fur's insulating properties were greatly beneficial during the bitterly cold winters.

Cavalier and Puritan, ca. 1645

The English cavalier (left) is dressed in a costume typical of the aristocracy and the wealthy, with a gaily colored silk, satin, or velvet jacket and matching breeches, decorated with braid. Accessories include a lace falling band, cuffs, and boot hose tops; a cloak; plumed swashbuckler's hat; gloves; and bucket-topped boots with butterfly spur shields. The Puritan on the right wears the typical "playne" clothes in "sadde" colors of his peers, although his cape could be of scarlet wool.

Lower-middle-class Puritans, ca. 1640

This farmer couple has come to town to peddle their wares. Their costumes are more reflective of the general look of the Puritans, who avoided the ornamentation of upper-class fashions. Sleeves with but a single slash were considered acceptable, as on the man's shirt. The woman's bodice was probably a wealthy person's used garment which had not yet had the braid removed to reflect Puritan modesty.

Royalist soldiers and farm girl, ca. 1642–45

A royalist militiaman (left) and pikeman (right) receive refreshment from a farm girl.
The pikeman wears red-and-white sleeves as part of his uniform.

Cromwellian musketeer and pikeman, ca. 1642–45

This musketeer and pikeman worked under the Parliamentarian cause, which supported the Protestants in their bid for religious freedom in England. Under the leadership of Oliver Cromwell, an influential general and statesmen, the Protestants overthrew the monarchy in the English Civil Wars, also known as the Great Rebellion. The musketeer (left) is using a support fork to aid in firing his musket. His bodice and breeches are padded for protection, and small gunpowder cases hang from his bandolier. The pikeman (right) wears body armor over a red-and-black shirt.

Oliver Cromwell with Parliamentarian couple, ca. 1646

Cromwell (left) confers with a Parliamentarian official and his wife. As befitting the Puritan ethic, they all wear somber-toned clothing, but Cromwell and the Parliamentarian sport red sashes as a sign of their office.

Puritan refugees in flight, ca. 1645

The English Civil Wars took place between 1642 and 1651, pitting the Royalists against the Parliamentarians. As with many wars, the confiscation of property and danger forced people to find refuge far from home, as with this farmer couple. Their clothing shows their lower-class background, which was in line with humble Puritan ethics. Since frugality was considered a virtue, patching one's clothing for extended use was commendable. The baby is wrapped in swaddling bands, a common practice then that might be considered cruel today.

Wealthy English Puritan couple, ca. 1650

The Puritans and the Parliamentarian cause were not without resources, having control of London, the prosperous south and east areas of England, and most of the ports. The lady is wearing a white eyelet embroidered falling band and cuffs, with her dark wool skirt caught up in her waistband to expose a silk underskirt with ribbon banding. The gentleman is wearing a conservative version of Rheingraves under a slashed jerkin, with shirtsleeves in red and black stripes. His bucket-topped boots have interesting stirrup covers, which suggest flattened ribbons.

English Puritans, ca. 1650

This couple faithfully follows the strict Puritan code for "playne" dress, with a noticeable absence of decorative accessories and ornamentation. The tall hats and dark fabrics are typical telltale traits of a Puritan costume.

Oliver Cromwell made "Lord Protector," ca. 1653

Following his defeat of the Stuart monarchy, Oliver Cromwell (1599–1658) was made lord protector of England, Scotland, and Ireland, ensuring him a virtual dictatorship until his death. Though he was ostensibly advised by a reformed Parliament, he dissolved the body more than once upon encountering opposition. Cromwell sought to establish a strong Puritan church in England, but was tolerant of other denominations of Christian worship. Though often vilified, his leadership inarguably strengthened his country's stature. Here, Cromwell wears body armor with the red Parliamentary sash of office.

Dutch regent siblings, ca. 1650

Taken from a painting of the children of a wealthy Protestant regent, this illustration demonstrates Dutch conservatism in fashion. The styles shown were first introduced in the court of Louis XIII in 1633, with the male outfit being the precursor to the dashing cavalier look. The young man's suit is of a muted-color satin with lace trim and ribbon rosettes, which could tighten or loosen the waistband. The girl's gown is of somber-colored satin with a lace-edged neckline and ribbon rosettes at the waistband and at the elbow of the slashed, puffed sleeves.

King Charles II and Princess Mary of Orange, ca. 1660

Charles II (1630–1685, son of the executed Charles I) was exiled to continental Europe while Cromwell and the Puritans ruled his homeland. He was restored to the throne shortly after Cromwell's death, and brought with him a taste for French fashion. Here he is seen dancing with his sister, Mary Stuart (1631–1660), mother of the future English king, William III. Charles wears Rheingraves and the shortened jacket, both bedecked with ribbon loops and bows. Mary's gown is simple in cut and features a falling band from neck to elbow.

Louis XIV and court lady, ca. 1660

King Louis XIV wears the French version of Rheingraves with a short jacket. Louis (1638–1715) ushered in a political golden age for France, though he mercilessly persecuted his Protestant subjects. He turned his love of beauty into a political tool, as well as a source of great wealth for the royal court, by encouraging a national "brand" of lavish luxury. This was especially practiced in the art of fashion, as can be seen in the lady's gown with its divided skirt and low-cut neckline, the height of fashion for this time and decidedly un-Puritan. Wired curls and falling tendrils complete the look.

New Amsterdam Puritans, ca. 1655

The Dutch founded New Amsterdam in 1624 on the island of Manhattan and made it a profitable trading center. A number of Puritans from Holland settled there and along the Hudson River. They brought with them the Dutch version of simple costume and muted colors, as illustrated here. In 1664, the English seized the colony and renamed it New York.

Seventeenth-century French peasants

Throughout the century, the dress of the French peasants reflected their unfortunate lot in life. Eking out an existence as best they could with limited means and opportunities, they generally pieced clothing together from rags from the scrap bin. The Puritans looked to them as an example of the wrongs brought about by the monarchy.

New Amsterdam merchant and lady, ca. 1660

This illustration shows a successful New Amsterdam merchant and his lady, a class that was quickly becoming landed gentry in the New World. They built estates along the Hudson River just before the English takeover of the colony on the island of Manhattan. They continued to avoid ostentation by wearing dark colors in the Puritan manner, although modest ornamentation was widely used.

Dutch merchant and lady, ca. 1660

A young merchant wears a much more tailored version of Rheingraves, with a jacket and cloak also stripped of excessive decoration. His lady wears a dark gown with a broad white collar; under her skirt, a red petticoat is revealed.

Dutch upper-class man, ca. 1660

The Dutch version of the cavalier fashion was less flamboyant than that of the French and English, though still recognizable. This young man wears a dark cloak, jacket, and Rheingraves, accessorized with dark stockings, shoes, and hat—with plumes conspicuously absent.

Dutch upper-class lady, ca. 1660

This young lady wears a gown in pale satin with a bodice that dips in front like a stomacher. Her three-quarter-length sleeves end with the cuffs of her white camisole turned back. The gown's skirt matches the bodice and sleeves in color, and has a front panel and trim of gold lace. The lady's hair is pulled back into a bun with curled tendrils hanging down the sides of her face.

English nobleman and son, ca. 1663

This family lived during the English Restoration period, which began with the installation of Charles II to the throne following Cromwell's death. The nobleman wears Rheingraves with justaucorps (a knee-length coat inspired by military styles). Every available surface is covered with decoration, which included gold embroidery, lace, ribbons, and brocaded fabrics. His young son's costume also consists of Rheingraves, but worn with a shorter jacket and cloak. Multicolored ribbon loops and bows highlight the boy's brightly colored satin garments. A falling band of plain white features collar ties of gold thread.

English noblewoman and children, ca. 1663

The mistress of the family wears a brightly colored velvet bodice and skirt over a lawn chemise, with a petticoat in a silk of contrasting hue. A ladder of ribbons called an échelle fastens her bodice closure and the slits of her sleeves. The little girl wears a silk gown with a closed bodice and open overskirt in a light color. Her white lawn collar was also known as a "whisk" or "band." The little boy in the walker wears a brimmed cap over a fitted lawn cap. His short-sleeved, long-skirted gown is of brightly colored silk, while his band and chemise are of white lawn. Little boys wore skirts until they reached five or six years of age.

English gentlemen, ca. 1666

During the Restoration period, which lasted nearly three decades, the style sported by the gentleman on the left—which consisted of Rhinegraves with a short jacket—fell out of favor. Charles II introduced the "Persian" mode, worn by the gentleman on the right. A long coat and long vest was worn over narrow knee breeches, a look that was soon adopted and adapted throughout the continent.

French nobles, ca. 1680

Louis XIV took the rather simple "Persian" outfit favored by Charles II and transformed it into a work of splendor.
Layers of gold-embroidered cloth, topped by the full-bottomed wig, quickly became the model of high fashion. The
lady wears a hairstyle and cap ensemble called a "fontange," inspired by one of his mistresses. Her jacket blends
into the manteau (overskirt) to form a train. The lace design appliquéd on her skirt is called "pretintailles."

Ladies from the English Restoration period, ca. 1685

The ascension to the throne of James II (1633–1701), a Roman Catholic, fueled Protestant fears of intolerance and suppression. The last of the Stuart monarchs, he ruled for three years before being deposed by the Glorious Revolution in 1688. The fashions of the aristocracy and the Puritans changed little during this time, as illustrated by the gowns of these ladies.

English-American Puritans, ca. 1660

With James II as king, the fear of renewed religious persecution prompted some Puritans to depart for the New World, where they would be free to worship as they pleased. The first Pilgrims arrived at Plymouth, Massachusetts in 1620, where they established the first permanent colony in New England. The garments worn by this couple are typical of those that were worn by the Puritan colonists.

Puritan in stocks, ca. 1660

The Puritans strictly abided by their austere rules, and any infraction, including a violation of the dress code, could result in public humiliation. This man has been locked into stocks for a certain period of time as punishment for a misdeed. The stocks were often placed in a public location where passersby could lecture or mock the wrongdoers for their actions.

Upper-middle-class Pilgrim family, ca. 1674

Some English Puritans, especially from the merchant class, settled in Boston and amassed much wealth in the New World. Though this is a Puritan family, the tenets of simplicity and austerity seem to have been abandoned by the mother in favor of pearls, a lace-trimmed cap and collar, and appliquéd lace on her petticoat. The long ribbons hanging from the shoulders of the children were called "ribbons of childhood," and were popular in Europe and America for a brief time. The father is dressed in more traditional Puritan garb.

Salem witch trial, ca. 1692

The religious hysteria of the Salem witch trials was the harbinger of the end of the Puritan movement in America. Here we see a minister acting as chief justice, dressed in a somber suit with a neck cloth and red stockings, topped by a red cloak with gold embroidery on the collar. A midwife points to a mole or mark on the body of an accused witch, which was sufficient proof of collusion with the devil. In the background is a soldier with a neck hook to guide the witch along, so that she may not touch and thereby contaminate him. It was not until 1957 that the names of the last of the executed were legally cleared of any wrongdoing.

c.1610

c.1610

c.1610

c.1610

c.1620

c.1630

c.1635

c.1635

c.1635

c.1635

c.1635

c.1640

c.1650

c.1647

c.1647

c.1643

c.1650

c.1655

c.1660

Dutch hats and hairstyles of the seventeenth century

41

English Civil War hats and hairstyles of the cavaliers and Parliamentarians, ca. 1642–48

c.1660

c.1660

c.1660

c.1660

c.1660

c.1670

c.1670

c.1660

c.1660

c.1670

c.1670

c.1690

c.1680

c.1670

Tom Tierney c.1690

English Restoration and French court hats and hairstyles, ca. 1660–90

Various Puritan headwear and collars (English, American, and Dutch) of the seventeenth century

A variety of seventeenth-century shoe styles